IN
OUR
NAME

IN
OUR
NAME

POEMS

CURT G. CURTIN

Library of Congress Control Number: 2024906127

ISBN: 979-8-89228-107-2   (Paperback)
ISBN: 979-8-89228-108-9   (eBook)

Book Ordering Information:
Atticus Publishing
548 Market St PMB 70756
San Francisco, CA 94104
(888) 208-9296
info@atticuspublishing.com
www.atticuspublishing.com

Printed in the United States of America

Dedicated to the Refugees from war:

Cambodia, Laos, Rwanda, Uganda,
Congo, Kosovo, Sudan, Iraq, Ukraine, Gaza…
wherever on earth the innocents are made victims
of arrogance, equivocation and ignorance of war.

Acknowledgements

The following poems in this collection have been published previously:

"Girl of Darfur," Second Prize, Connecticut Poetry Society, 2019, published in The Connecticut Review, 2020.

After Auden's "Musée des Beaux Arts," First Prize, Frank O'Hara Award, Worcester County Poetry Association, 2010; published in The Worcester Review, Vol. XXXI, 1-2, 2010. Also received the editor's 2010 nomination for a Pushcart Prize, and reprinted in For Art's Sake, Kelsay Books, 2019. "Man Achieves Flight," was also published in For Art's Sake.

"Item" and "Kwan Yin's Eyes" published in The Other Side of Sorrow: Poets Speak Out About Conflict, War, and Peace, Poetry Society of New Hampshire, 2006; the collection won the 2007 Independent Publisher's Book Award, Bronze Prize.

"The Voice of a Slave," published in Diner, 2006.

Several of the poems have previously appeared in chapbooks produced by the author: Elusive Music (2005) and Embers Carried Across the River in a Gourd (2015)

CONTENTS

Preface

The story of Job is a fable, an illustration of a theme common to humanity. There is the great question: If we are the special darlings of a good, just, omniscient and omnipotent god, then why is there so much apparently undeserved, and often inhumane suffering? Why is evil allowed to enter our lives? Perhaps this is a test of what use we make of power. In Job the false counselors are unwise, use their reasoning power to feed their egos. Job is torn between awe of Yahweh and anger with His persecution of him. Now, if there may be no god, where does Job's condition and his rebellion direct itself? In these poems, I explore themes of violence with the aid of secular and religious thought from many sources over many centuries. That is the work of this book.

DREAMS FROM EDEN

I remember yellow grass, fragile light
on butterflies, world within a seeming
tranquil sky. Then a dark winged eagle
wheeled and swiftly dove to kill a mole.
Innocent as art I took the vision in
remembering with childlike eyes and
mole's blood dripping from my chin.

I wonder at illusions now, this and others
that I find in dreams. At times I hear
a music whole, in harmony and radiance—
three sides, I'm told, of beauty's face.
Then underneath, a contrapuntal phrase
that wills all graces to be still while some
bright eyes compose a predatory will.

Father and Sons

Cain gave the Lord plain farmer's fare
raised by sweat of his brow;
Abel gave the first born lamb.
The Lord told Cain He had respect for Abel,
none at all for Cain;
"And Cain was very wroth,"
the Bible said, "and his countenance fell."

Well sure, the kid was pissed,
being dissed by the biggest
Guy around. Still, being dissed is
damned poor cause to kill. But then
there's this: isn't it also true
the Lord was a cause of jealousy?
Extenuating circumstance?
Lord knows, I guess you'd say.
So Cain, already an alien, was
driven forever away—even though
he had no priors I could find.

This is what I learned beneath a tree:
the Lord, in those days, loved
a sacrifice; so you might say that
Abel played it right; a lamb was
just the untried, innocent thing
to catch the meaning of the King.
Or you could say poor stupid Cain
tried hard to learn by his example,
chose the closest sacrificial lamb
     and so was damned.

THE LASH ARRIVES

The earth is a ragged animal that moves
more lightly than you think. Some few
have heard its voice complaining where
it runs across desolate space, sometimes
howling into the gray air on the edges of
cities. Deeper under the sea than anyone
goes that rugged skin begins to shred.
On the Rockies, Alps and Kush it feels
irritation along the spine, and the heat
running down now burns the sides.

We think it has no master, but it has—
the Lash fitted with powerful claws that
tear the moss from rock to find a tasty mite,
the Lash that came down from the trees
wielding a vigorous mind.

The earth is a ragged ball that moves
more lightly than you think, lightly, lightly
growing weak, ever since the Lash arrived.

OTHERS

Strange books light the *others'* ways,
they play tanbur or samisen, harmonica,
they wear fur hats, eat quantities
of cabbage, garlic, curried rice,
speak not exotic but anomalous tongues.
The *other* come from Rift and Indus,
altiplano, Haiti, house next door.
They set up little shops with upstairs flats.
The *other* are rich, the *other* are poor,
they praise another god than mine
or none at all. *They* are ugly, old or fat.
The *other* wear black, the *other* wear
rainbows and we think *they* sing all day.
The *other* are flamboyant, gay, or maybe
unable to read. The *other* are always asking
to be seen, always demanding dignity.
Uniquely, I see
what burden they place on me!

Beholders

Hell is arrogance ingenerate in war,
littleness in strident mouths
filling the cancerous belly of today
devouring generations for the wealth
of blood and gold with no knowledge of
their souls, appetite of incendiary fist
and will, fed on suppurating ego
festering in an empty grail, and

Hell is the many-celled eye that looks away
while massacre the little ones becomes
a planned design of war; on TV, mothers
pulling furniture and babes in ragged carts,
we see wars of old women in old shoes
leaving home in the snow, see whole tribes
in the dry and treeless heat starving,
all those festering eyes, enumerated ribs
and bellies rising where there is no bread.
In hell they speak of policy, of interests
conflicting, of the way to balance bread and
a budget; this is how the many-celled eye looks,
and

Hell is ignorance seeking itself
down well-known streets broad signs identify
like smoke that just denotes
without a spark, without imagination;
we have heard them in the coffee shops, wise
as tethered lions following speakers leading
mown avenues of monstrous thought
made small enough to please. These

are among the enablers, drink unthinking
from the empty grail, and blink
in the confusing light of the many-celled eye

I tell you, blind eyes, heaven bent, torn eyes
of sorrow-taught wanderers amid confusion and heat
keep wonder alive for the inner eye. Deep within
the suffering show, the sin is in our eyes.

WIRING

In Boston, Massachusetts
the Six-year-old squats
facing Five-year-old. Together
and alone these babies play,
content within a moment,
until a moment when—and it
could only have been a moment,
not a thought or a plan,
and surely too early for Satan—
when unsuspecting Six
in sudden undecided motion
punched the inoffensive Five,
who ran crying for the bosom
of the woman out of sight.

Now Six, for the very first time
contemplating (more than thinking,
less than prayer) his sin of power,
how strange that his fist, *He*, struck
that inoffensive face of Five.

BREEDING

It isn't right
to go for the throat
in hasty hate
like a trucker whose mother's been cursed;

elegant spite,
perverse and polite,
is patiently nursed
like a dark Transylvanian thirst.

Basic Training

Sure we played at guns, but that
was fantasy from news and movies
far removed from fear. Real fear,
in little doses, was meeting
on the street another kid who
looked (he knew he did) tougher
than you. Admiration of size,
height, swagger, the arm of boys
you knew or didn't know at all,
just passing by, was daily fare.

We grew, and so did awe
in the presence of beef or talk
that measured mean on scales
beyond our daily need, beyond
real knowledge of ourselves.
Compensatory reckoning
became a part of each day's walk
for men in harmony with men.
We're a little ashamed in a world
that advertises big and mean
to be both virtue and virility.

It's quite a bore after a certain age,
this boyish need that shapes too much
of life, makes us prey to shapers
who design our wars and sell us
into muscle cars. I am offended by
the innocent, unnatural walk of boys
who seek to be seen as mean, men
who make a heavy portrait of themselves
to keep the ingrained fear out of reach.
Blessed be the meek.

STREET SCENE

He believes he has himself designed
shoulders sinewy as boars' thighs.
I have seen his restless dreams
of dangerous streets, the unseen thing
that makes of his heroic nights
erection of that mirrored wall,
seminal sinewy shadow of fear.

Late Spring brings the circling falcon,
Summer the charging boar;
power in fear of fear begins
a running in the spleen, the viscera
of terrible machines howling in
the tongues of young men and their guns.

Ah, the older ones who use them to effect
their other dreams that are made within
the market and are told with bland deceit;
there's a brotherhood of terror in our
dreams, and when we see the bloody error
we are followed by another round of dreams.

WHITE BOY, 1950

Hilt down for an easy slide from under the sleeve,
the only white boy in the yard—everybody
busted ass for the yard boss, yeah, and another
upstairs, unseen, just the white Cadillac.

Luke did time for murder, Jazz was jailed in Alabama.
Submarine and Bob and Stoke could only read streets,
and One White Boy down on his luck in Boston,
freedom's cradle, and colored stay in your place.
So we loaded trucks without a lift gate. Backs.
I walked the walk that said I'm hard and cool. Fool.

So when I called him out on the loading dock,
Stoke looked down at me as dark as storm.
Of course I knew—tensed from arm to asshole.
He leaped, together we in sweat we worked
each other over, yard boss waiting out of sight.
Others hung against the dock, cool and easy.

All day long, arm to arm, lifting barrels filled
with scrap, non-ferrous brass or copper.
We tip the barrels back, squat, one hand each
grip the bottom rim, each, link each other's arms
behind the barrel and lift. Barrel's lip must catch
the edge of truck bed, then we shoulder on.
It couldn't be done alone.

But then the fight. The knife slipped out
of my sleeve. Big black Dan, the only friend
I'd made in this dark place, picked it up.

When it was over Dan gave back the knife.
"Why? he said." Shame came on me then.
I carry it still like a hidden blade.
          White boy. Why?

DREAMS

Those flawed underground gods, they work
a wide and resonating tomb. At times I have
descended, moved through dreams they sent
to melt defense. Leaving will behind, my
numbed mind went down. There I saw
angelic faces, their bodies gnarled and twisted
like roots of ancient trees. Without a word they
beckoned me, and their smiles were terrible to see.
Their vault is high, hung with noble heraldry
and licenses of many kinds, their history of little
tyrannies. Litter covers the floor: dolls, blackboards,
belts and rope, hymnals worn from heavy use, apron
hung on a kitchen chair; ordinary things. Ceremony
attends: a brief procession, then the blessing of the dark
by which they see.

They hover over children brought to the crypt
by innocent means, and they sing like hawks
as they fold their wings around the dreams
they find in each child's eyes. Often
they love the child with a special intensity.
One child kneels, as if in supplication,
one hand on the stove.
Sobbing is heard from a closet.
Another, having had his turn,
is now asleep and dreaming,
fearing to go outside.

When the children leave, they keep these dreams,
weave them into the night of secret defeats.

Fear

Fear is the deer's salvation,
stillness and ears that hear a seed fall,
and when the determined dogs arrive
she tires them beautiful running—
though they catch and divide her mother.

If only the world were thickets and trees,
if only the children had powerful legs
to outrun the dogs of war—if only
their mothers did too. But the dogs
are run by hunters in hidden designs
and the guns they love are stronger than
anyone's fear can be, and the mother and
child are on their knees when the dogs arrive.

POWER

1
A full-grown German Shepherd stands
astride a groveling Basset hound,
with brutish might, dominates.
The sun shines equally on each, and that
won't be controlled; the dish is always filled
enough for two, and neither knows how to
unlock the gate. The top dog seems to need
the bottom dog. If his desire is overmuch
indulged, the little hound dies;
best allow some room for licking wounds.

2
He was gone again, away in rage,
he slams the door, his 4X4 roars
like another snarling beast.
At the vanity her beauty things, blush
and such, restore small grace where
the split lip bled or places raised
in blue-black shadowing,
her delicate as love touch.
She knows that in the night
a boy with a winsome grin will
come again, possibly bearing creams
to seal the woman in.

CONTROL

I have seen a world of wars
where wisdom was not enough
to redeem the tortured design,
seen the frenzied beasts that feed
within our eyes, grow blind
and arrogantly show the way
wearing all the sacred robes
and roles, the little flags that
sanctify these horrors that we
spin from deep within. This
is how we sin.

Fortitude may be enough
to keep the mind from an abyss
where falling is all there is,
but that is not enough to fathom
hate and fear that drives
the fearsome warriors who hack
the babies in their mothers' arms,
herd the elders dying by the road,
destroy in flames unholy others,
and later wear the ribbons in
a silly parade to the grave
old age.

What a catalog I could make
from this little sight my years allow.
So many of us have made this list
as if that act could exorcise the beast,
leaving only virtues we have also seen,
charity and love that made us cry
thinking the gods could be kind after all.

FLIGHT

In the tower seat under the wide gull wing,
I sang alone the lift of landlost air, smiled
at my reflection in a porthole far above
the pulse of a planet's ocean. How easy
seems a world can be left behind, as if it
were never a cage some god had made.

Memory is another god: a will to knit time
and history, a seeming endless energy that
will provide. What then of a moment from
a warplane's sky revised in adolescent ego,
a moment blind to 50's mounted in the waist,
twin-30's in the nose, bombsight in the tail?

That was long ago, days of windsong out of
hearing now. Stealthy as a night owls' flight,
reflections since have cast a different light:
some radiance that works within, some dark
that does the same; works and ways from
whence our judgment and the judgment of
the world is made to work its' dark finality.

MAN ACHIEVES FLIGHT

The cock's dark eyes awake in flight his wide
shrieks warning
shocks to come exempt no one. Sleep
children sleep

> Dresden
> where the children melted
> Sleep children sleep

> Hiroshima, Nagasaki
> human imprints on the street
> Sleep children sleep

> Vietnam napalm
> running girl screaming
> Sleep children sleep

Saturday night black raptors screech.   Sleep
children sleep, it's
only the sound of backyard fowl in a sick dream
shrieking
only earth of feverish green and orange fright-ignited
skies
only a beast come in the night waking innocence
to die

Based on the painting "Guernica" by Pablo Picasso. The bombing of Guernica
by German and Italian air forces was the first time civilian populations were
targeted for bombing. Well known among the many bombings of civilians after
that were the fire-bombing of Dresden in WWII, the first use of atomic bombs
in Hiroshima and Nagasaki, and the first use of napalm bombing in Vietnam.

Serbian Nurses, 1999

Dressed in uniforms of white
Serbian nurses enlisted Infancy
in war with weaponry of rude embrace,
abuse, neglect and hate. Witness eyes
of babies' fright when caring wears
a nurses' angry eyes. Instead of white
a loathsome veil fell across millennia
of holy expectation. Naked in a tribal
war, sympathy and nurturing decay
where innocence is prey of hate.

Report from Serbia: Serbian nurses hate, neglect and abuse Albanian babies.

THE BAMIYAN BUDDHA

The Bamiyan Buddha does not heed
the hammers of the Taliban; dynamite
does not intrude on his serenity.
These things are unholy, angry traffic
in the marketplace, mingled with the
rabid cries of restless men who fear
a world not one but many, fear to
set their anger and anathemas aside
to hear the pleas of Buddhists who
may teach the angry how to read.

News item: In March 2001, Taliban leaders decree destruction of ancient Buddha
and of all religious icons, saying they are forbidden by the Koran.

THE AFGHAN WOMEN

Cover your virtues
or be stoned.
In the master's sight
avert your eyes—lights
known to see a man's
loose flank, wrinkled knee,
his little prides hung in dumb
sterility—He only loves
his guns.
Deep within he knows
that a god's power lies
with woman great with life.
Never wonder why,
veiled in laws of a merciful god,
merciless men alone decide:
your release would bring demise
to power in an empty sac
and lies that veil his eyes.

One Year After 9/11

Only the cameras, mute, can speak,
our tongues still held in disbelief.
Two planes filled with innocents but
piloted by hate shattered massive towers,
and brought them to the street. Here
was a dream scene filtering through vivid sleep
that crushed complacency and peace.

From afar we watch the gritty smoke, together
and alone, we, still choking on this misery.
All day and night our sad eyes sighted on
heaps of dying where men scaled ragged sides,
sent from within to find a human voice alive.

Immensity dawns in tangle of blood and stone
and stories deep in memory's faces. They repeat:
the holy names, the saddened families, homes
where they are known for long years coming.
There were no strangers on those streets.
We will ourselves a second sight, mourners
torn from lasting grief to watch again
the shifting heap where underneath
so many were still and dead.
And on this day we open mouths to speak,
only echoes come of every other's grief.

THE CITY ON THE HILL
(November, 2004)

On land the golden wheat is aflame,
sheaves we bound with honest dreams,
torches lit with earth's black yield.
The eagle wheels above the smoke
unable to see what lies below.
We race all wheels to be free
from the reek of burning soil, race
smoke blind, to the shining sea.

There the cruise ships ply where fog is lit by dreamy lights,
the harbor far from sight. We dine, the table graced with
tarts and plums. Acquisitions fill the state rooms.
The industry of indifference flickers on supple screens
where sirens air their idiot songs. Over the din, we hear
the sound of a distant tide; it frightens us into superfluous
might that does not stop the children crying. We strain
in noisy shallows to be heard over the distant, dying
voices, codas of so many falling songs.

This ship pitches in troubled seas, blunders through with
shocks of thoughtless cruelty. Electronic blips are missed,
we fail to see our Scylla and Charybdis:
power that turns the rudder away, greed
that eats the keel; dice in the game room,
arrogant pilots plotting their stars below.
We navigate compensatory reckonings in
seas where systems drift, where ebb and
flow is counted, counted. Polymath, we
engineer no hatch for release
          of raven and dove.

THE HOLY LAND

Over the Mount of Olives circles a bright-eyed hawk,
merciless Paraclete guarding memorial stones.
Pity all small things foraging in the sun, for
this hawk holds no hope for living or dead,
is an unyielding symbol of will.

There is too much courage;
it is spilled all over the cafe floor,
it is clotting on shattered streets,
Rorschach shapes baked in the sun,
read each by each as prophecy.

There is too much faith,
god's eye raging in wrenched faces
screaming sacred hate
that spills tomorrow
on the red, weeping street.

Word, you are written on the land overrun
with heroes and saints, all gods' patriots.

If only it were only a piece of earth where
children play beneath the olive rows and
all tongues bargain in the marketplace.
Instead, it is a circling hawk, history relived
as ritual, unable to will escape.

Please, it is time for the *deus ex machina,*
the blessing of bloodless gods.

WONDER OF BLINDED EYES IN GAZA

Gaza, shaped like a dagger above the Gulf of Aqaba,
wind and grit honed blade that splits the east;
that place and a faithless woman once
imprisoned an eyeless man.
When that man understood his chains and rose
another temple came to ground.*

Many in our time have wandered eyeless in Gaza.
Those who look with wounded souls howl
at their incessant sense of loss;
their knives find enemies
among themselves, and sympathies they
wash away with blood.

All the deserts are aligned with tribes; even
the sands become the color of tongues, dry, dry
tongues raw with words of certainty spitting dry
into the holy winds in ancient tongues.

____

Written in 2014; unfortunately still all too relevant.
*Samson.

The Voice of a Slave

is not heard with ear unattuned
to a rhythm of chains, where they ring on chastened bones.

On the grave where you wasted your pride you may throw
yourself down
and utter sane rage till the blooded tongue is undone.

You hold the column where organ tone trembles,
embrace the stone you have come to bring down. Alone,

you oppose in the bones.

Color

Africa is cut to the bone, self-inflicted
with knives annealed in northern forges,
machete memories that dissever tribes,
the lust of power that knows no brother,
selected pages of a prophet's book; then,
so many children born with wounds
their fathers bind with wounded memory.
These boils that rise and suppurate
are not allowed to heal; the women who
would lance them hide, or they be lanced
by roving, lawless men of every tribe.
Their sons become the generals who ride
in limousines; or bodies spent in killing,
killed. Fantastic flags call and justify.

Meanwhile, the progeny from ancient times
in lands most far above the equatorial line
watch with fogged binoculars. Some mourn
the women and children, some only the lost
romance of yesterday's pillage and safari.
Some count the ships that ply the seas between.
The pleas of NGOs light few candles where
great powers lie, in the whited manse and
arsenal or in houses where money holds
election; where the atlas, reconfigured,
maps the world in markets and waits.
Coiled within a thatch above the sleeper or
along a wandering vine a giant mamba waits.
The world, unwary, stores no antidote.

KWAN YIN'S EYES

In sleep I see a bird with Kwan Yin's eyes,
calm as long sorrowing. It utters no song.
That bird in flight flutters like a windblown leaf.
She means the world is stirred by thoughtless winds
that strip the trees and blow the nests away.

The bird is seeking sympathy in the lives
of troubled ones. I only know they are
the Other. We listen together to dry wind
droning on unfretted strings. The tanbur hangs
on a jagged wall, fragment of an empty home.

An old man and a child have walked away
with lost desire for strings, six days on broken roads
to a border where they are turned away.
Dry wind on strings, empty lamentation
for the soul of another undone home.

The bird with Kwan Yin's eyes flutters
in a wounded way. She means to say the world
is shattering like scenes on Chinese teacups
thrown against ancient walls, all the walls
where people write their border lines

in splintered tongues and shattered sight.
The bird with Kwan Yin's eyes alights
on the tanbur, her wings spread wide across
the silent strings. She means that loud
disharmonies of hate and war abide

in towns where tanbur, sitar and lute once
were heard in the homes and schools. Only
the wind now learns their unheard monodies.
Where are the children's fingers
that could play? They are stroking the dead,

they are holding wicked toys, they fly away.
The bird with Kwan Yin's eyes huddles
her wings and closes her eyes. She means
it is a long time, a passage through human
designs unraveling. The savage weds the savant

where there is no ceremony, nothing
but forward motion in immense disharmony.
In time the wind will subside, leaving
belief hanging like dry leaves waiting for spring,
waiting for children's fingers to play again.

Mockingbird

Twenty-thirty imitations, over an hour of borrowed song.
Ah, but it's not harmony that matters to him; it's mastery.
The mockingbird sings many tongues, loves just one.
He will attack the poor chick lured by song. So covetous
he will attack the long-tailed image in the window pane.
Territory and offense, false song and assault, rhythms
of a wilderness. Strange, the instruments we learn to fear.

Shall we practice angry anthems everywhere, with
a harsh cry claim all fat berries hung on a distant bush,
all the watering places, even the air as far as we can see?
The lark and sparrow complain, take greater risk
after wintering too long. They will carry wicked mirrors,
tear at nests of others and their own, till over the fence
hung rich with fruit the locust horde comes in.

ITEM

He holds his mother, or somebody's mother
with wasted arms. How does he choose
among the mothers, all bony and gray
heaped in an open grave? *He only said
she looked as if she could be his.*

The reporter chokes at the sight, an open sore
that he cannot read as merely another item:
"Child Grieves in the Heart of Africa."
He takes the boy from numberless flies
and death in heaps, a scene that could fill
an inside page, and brings him to a hospital.

Next day when the reporter returns, hope in hand,
chocolate—that's what brings relief, ask any child
on your street, *Oh no*, they say, *that boy has died.*
But why? *He decided not to live any more,
and so he died.*

And so.
Too dry for tears, too dumb with grief, he chose;
and all the mothers, and all the others in that grave
drew the inconsolable child to their embrace

Where are the arms that made that grave?
They are cradled in secret understandings,
wrapped in blood-soaked flags,
nursed on the pap of lies and apathy.

Drawn by deadlines' press on a day like others
when so many strive for fame or die, we tire,
but do not decide to die. What is enough—
hugging his mother or one that could be—
enough to open a column with aid?

———————

Based on a 2004 story by a British reporter in The Congo.

GIRL BETRAYED

Behind a wall of twisted
vines, dark and green,
hatched thick with fear,
she folded in so,
a stunned bird fallen,
all the singing gone.

All green and dark
my blindness and my fear,
all ragged rage
those sounds that choke
 our severed tears.

GIRL OF DARFUR

Shall I kill this baby? God, I am asking you.
Each day I waver like palm in a hot wind.
This poor thing is innocent,
but I am so full of dirty shame, of hate
that wants her away from me
and still I desire to nurse her need. My splintered will.
No peace in this wounded will;
one way or the other, love or kill this little one
who came like knives of fire; it wasn't even lust,
those many laughing at brutality—I cannot say, only
again, again they took my body, beat
disgust into my soul.

You see, God? How can I decide
between innocence, hers and mine?
Did you send them?
Did they not have an arm like God
to reach me where I hid, to choose me, virgin girl?
She cries, poor thing. Hunger
is everywhere here. Her need. Mine—I would as soon die.
But this poor child, she is—no, not mine—
yes mine—and daughter of too many men
whose mix of blood and sperm found their evil way in me.

Oh God, she cries.
Why do I want to hold her, stop her tears with my old hymns—
but she looks too much like those: her eyes, her skin.
I am so angry that I cannot cry; but then, sometimes
the crying is the dry wind that howls from the desert.
It strangles my soul.
Whirlwind God, answer me now.

MOTHER

Mom
extant
in the hollow place

full of empty, still filled
with child
reaching for reaching for reaching m m mm
speech compressed
under stun
noooh noooh

silly sky all day hung brown veils
night sky wandering lights
sedative another

still a child yesterday
so bright at morning yesterday
silly at night yesterday
and so to bed nooh

HEEE HIDES
loathing no face I
cannot think act that he
nooh

dark evil damn dark,
nooh
nooh Oh God nooh
why did you make them so?

News Item: ten-year-old girl taken from her bed, used for sex, then killed
(If read aloud, ideally the poem should be read by a woman.)

HEART OF DARKNESS

Ships no longer shell the jungle canopy.
Freighters quietly slip alongside and lorries
haul from cities grown like calluses upon a
great brown body. The inner station's
held by rebels with rocket launchers, new men
with old sores and torn souls. On dark rivers
and sparse tarred roads that slide like snakes
through sand and jungle the old ways fade
into sightless tyrannies. Refugees flee to
where they fall under revolution's wheels,
children given guns in sunless jungle hideaways
fire manic exultation at the faultless sky.
Dear girls are sold from African ships, abused
in African ransom camps, babies are born
with HIV, and only the tse-tse fly retains old ways.
Generals and demagogues, crocodiles at
shriveled water holes, make faithless pacts with
northern traffickers to skim the green of Africa,
dig and flay the great brown skin to fill ribbed ships
that haul a desiccated continent away.
All others quarantine the Black Death in its rage
to keep "the horror" in its darkened cage.

No Wonder We Call It Hunger

There are thoughts we have not known
except in afterthought: satisfaction,
regret, retribution or love.
They wait nature's time and a dab of chance.
Consider the sweet appeal of innocence,
cause of tender love and bestial sacrifice;
know that the budding brimming youth,
confused, holds thoughts of cellared animus and saint;
even the priest, mother, sage, they are moved
from these deep places, and they sing love's praise,
and they carry whips to flagellate.

These are the impatient strands where
animals plead for life by a gnawing seed
that slips unseen from belly to brain.
Power hides in the guise of eros and it
dreams the whip alive. Dearness folds
in long embrace in that unencumbered
place where the blood is sweetly shared.

How survival coincides with reckless and
with loving aims is where the beast resides.
Tame the tiger and the lamb
but do not misread the man.

ICH UND DU

Ich und Du, we walk together
on the mountain where an eagle,
eyes clear as polished steel,
speaks of Other in raptor tongue.
At first it seems only shrieking.

But an owl and a raven reply,
and in their dialects we perceive
dark imaginings. First a bear,
then a tiger come to mind, each
one a vision of dread in the night.

When a hawk appears with a snake
writhing in his grasp and shrieks
that a nest is near, you and me, we
take to wing and with eyes like steel
search every hearth for the Other.

Ich und Du: title of a work by theologian, Martin Buber

MORNING SONGS

Sorrow hovers over shock,
unrest beneath speech in this or any other life
except each night's waking dream
can last for years, fail to resolve,
to bind cohesive form for months
when something akin to shock by
bone or blood rises, fire from fissure.
Gracious as an ape, snarling pain escapes.
It's nature.
There will be tomorrows. Oh. Oh

Hiding in a Lavatory Stall

We were not prepared for this boy, still a child, a mind
not fully grown, who could compel himself to kill
an unknown, unoffending other child. His history
only partly links him to us: autism, isolation,
and that he killed without remorse, so
far as we can know.

There are those who want revenge, a justice
swift, uncompromising, trial as an adult. That deepens
the mystery: justice, mental illness, because we could not
understand his mystery, or ours. I mean that we are linked
by possibility, by the strangeness we
also know dwells within.

What I want to know is how his suffering affects us all
in a place we hold apart, where we have some impotent
half-vision of our own mystery; and I want to know
that others care to search within a boy who searches
his own incomplete and dazed interior for connection
to a whirling world.

I want to see him grown aware, able to suffer memory and
compassion; but if his mental state is such that he cannot,
I want the rest of us to be compassionately wise, to set aside
our ancient retributions. If that may be
the only good that we can make of this,
let us try.

For John Odgren, his victim, James Alenson, and the
Unnamed Boy

July 4ᵗʰ In The Neighborhood

On an evening when the world is in a killing rage,
a thousand families bring their frisbees,
folding chairs and soda pop
to Christoforo Columbo Park
where the band is already playing patriotic songs.

The sky is alive in sudden color, bursts of flame,
shapes of trumpet lilies, poppies,
moments of dark between.
In the rockets' red glare mothers cuddle children
born since Desert Storm, *oooh* and *aaah*.

PARTNERS IN COMMERCE

Somewhere in the snow old women
in old shoes flee from home,
pull a cart with all they own;
somewhere in a dry and treeless heat
ribs and bellies rise
where there is no bread. There

we see the eagle and the jackal
trading prey, appetite
of covetous lust, interest
concealed by warlike cries,
treacle in a common cup
that sparrows gladly sip,
then twitter in the coffee shops,
tethered birds that speak of flags
and follow others' calls made
small enough to please.

Somewhere in the snow old women
in old shoes flee from home
pull a cart with all they own;
somewhere in a dry and treeless heat
ribs and bellies rise
where there is no bread.

Crazy for Freedom

1.

I'm just crazy about freedom,
about not being made to kneel or be
locked in breathless space.

In this, the asylum my father freely chose,
I keep asking about freedom—by which
I mean mine, and even yours—and can't
believe the response from Doctor Spinner
and his security staff, which is mainly,
"Make believe."

These are make believers making believe,
making *to* believe; which I will not do
if made to. But there it is, this place is
run by earnest practitioners, mis-speakers
and liars afflicted with sincerity—Does
that give me confidence—confidence
men and all-day-smilers who say we
have to liberate the oil of Evil Others?
Make believe.

This is exciting but not thrilling. I'm
always afraid the smilers are selling me
closets, secretly padding my knees. I fear
when they seem most sincere: "In God
we—but we're watching over you—
bless America," or when I hear them utter
prayers that take my breath away: "We
who are without sin will cast the lives of
millions in the layered schist of our belief."
Make believe.

2.

This place is a profitable business
with all sorts of disposable goods:
boys and girls friends and enemies
legal rights sacred honor and trust
God bless our beautiful swift words
mine eyes have seen the glory of the
gory war machine oh say can you slip
slick rigs into that hallowed ground

Our boys over there and over and over
                    over there don't you dare say no to
                              weapons of mass democracy sincerely
yours.

POSSIBILITY

In our name, We, the state, embrace war without
a true account of outcomes, naming only the sins
of enemies, hiding our gains behind a wall of flags.
Perplexed by this deceit, we trust the secret state.
Even the mothers ululate or decorate their windows
when the belly of the state is great with war, though
civil paths become all bog and mud wash in a flash.

We have at hand the open book of understanding.
Look, look where the paths were made into roads
where streets were lit for walks on summer nights.
Look to echoes of creation in illuminated pages,
all things made to uncover the beauty within,
all places where we seek our hearts, whether
in work or song. Seek the sympathetic voice
breathing asylum in the churches and the laws.
Feel the peace we learned of bread given in need.
So much in common among these things, the
wide imagination writ not in One but many Books.

To unleash the shadow potency of *We*, we
must at least give cause beyond a demon's name,
beyond uncertain fear; we
must speak like people bent on hearing, hear
like people bent on seeing.

ROMANCE OF THE LOVESICK WARRIORS

Slender gun with sleek black barrel,
clips that lock with a sharp snap,
grip that licks my warm caress,
trigger that I gently press.

Caress my cheek black bride of death,
then on my arm you glide to rest,
while I rehearse you dreaming me
in my dark wedding best.

Steady I approach the altar, lovesick
and alone, potent venom mixed with ice,
there in sunless light, in cool control,
I gently hold my deadly soul.

And where are their smiling faces now,
their eyes that always seemed to know?
You see, so like a cat I crouch, control,
protect the underbelly of my soul.

———————

On the sick attraction of guns to men and boys

Stone

I descended a holy crypt and smashed some idols there.
Whether *trailing clouds of glory* or the open light of an
innocent mind my child rebelled against the whips and
goads, all the thoughtless drone that numbs a growing
soul. But how exhume the ghost of glory? What spirit
moves these undone bones *out of joint and wounded*?
Below the catafalque must be another door opens into
mystery, and I must heave the lid aside, past beads and
shroud and bones to the coiled ring that opens the stone.

I pondered why and how, read histories of ancients and of
cells more ancient still in Cenozoic stone. Among the lost,
their faith and need, all that hope for infinite connection,
some sympathy I knew, but not their shudder of awe.

The ring still holds me with its braided why and how. Is that
all there is, the ring of an endless question after another door,
the piling on of bones? Meaning to become *very wise,*
to place eternity in chains, I grip the twisted ring like an icon
of my own and am reminded of another's eternal stone.

---

trailing… Wordsworth
out of joint… Jacques Maritain
very wise: Sisyphus *(se-sophos)*

THE PATRIOT

The name is Thomas, plain and honest,
seeker into wounds; not to be sure of blood—
that is found everywhere these days—only
to inquire about signatures, signs,
evidence of deception.
Though I am a man of plentiful imperfections,
trust must be tested by sinners who care.

The spear always has a hand and the hand a voice.
When the voice utters ideals, beliefs,
denials and justifications, I say,
Put your finger upon each certainty,
see that it goes through to the bone.

Some of the wounds I seek to feel will not yield,
wrapped in gauzy tape by doctors, held
in prophylactic space. Seekers
are thought to be septic, cause of suppuration
in the public air, and Herod's men are everywhere.
But I do care, and care must carry a voice.
lest we bury innocents everywhere.

NIGHT

Awake at 3AM, leaving a dream that
slips away like Ariel into a tree, I turn to
a burden of memory. With practiced ease
it slides into this isle between heavy sleep
and day where these Erinyes insist on
being heard. I'm aware I'm cast alone,
no gods assigned to argue for me.

How shall I speak into their shrieks? Oh,
I have words enough to throttle a judge,
and I speak searchingly, ask in intricate
detail, time after time, of what is done
and by whom and why. Dry constriction
in my throat and loathing smother me.
I cease to speak. The judge decides upon
continuance, as he has done night after
night and will until the end of time.

JOHN

When I was a boy a near friend died
in the electric chair. He shot, killed
a lawman while escaping in a stolen car.
Escaping; magical thinking. He had a gun;
magical thinking. He was, and knew it, bright.
That meant—but he died of shock one night.
I'm 90 now. He's still mine.

MONUMENTS

Together-set-apart, we are brown or red or white,
Semite, Serb or Hashemite, speak Latino, Quebecois,
dialect of Hindi, and all have heavens full of gods
holier than thine. Leaders manipulate these in the
service of greed and send the children to war. They
tell us there is justice in their predatory aims and sell
our wars to children in the language of our games,
and after make a dead men's park and great parades
to elevate the moment and prepare us for another day.

Where are the monuments to all the babies slain?
Shall we pile the empty cradles on the soldiers' graves?
Where are the monuments to how our hatreds grew?
Are they etched in stone within our homes and holy places?

THOUGHTS THAT PASS THROUGH BORDERS

I remember brilliant colors-smells-laughter,
Saharan dust in the open markets, copper pots
and copper hands. I squat by a fire, am given
the chicken's heart to eat. That was long ago, before
the raking of coals. I thought only time had passed,
but the markets are overrun with guns. Angry hearts
have come from dust.

Unquiet night arrives in potent voices: a poisoned well,
renamed streets, a claim of ancient descent, poverty,
revenge, remembrance of a distant sin. Black, white
or copper, each against the other. Nation, tribe
and sect insist, their fears redeemed in speeches.
Official lies provide mythology for restless boys.
Imagination also dies.

There is that within us each, though more and less,
that needs the flame, life and death in fierce embrace
like a passionate lover who kills the other.

After the final blood,
after far too much of everything is spent, we ease
the weary mind, declare parades, nation exempt
from blame, honor the new economy, busy, busy.
Along the street the people agree: pretense of
remembrance, passwords, harmony of silent eyes,
all flags that have passed this way before,
unlettered speech easy to the tribal tongue.
Already too late the memorial stones.

Trust

Rwanda
The boys are led to sleep in the schoolroom
and wait for the friendly troops to arrive.
There is blood on the floor and blood on
the walls. The troops have blood in their eyes.

Colombia
Again she asks, do police know where
he lies. They laugh and say he must be gone
or hidden away. The little girl sees their eyes
and their shovels are wet with clay.

Congo, Angola, Kenya, Lybia...

THE STATE, IT IS ME

Product of force, accident, accretion, nurture, need,
sex and symbiosis turning in orbits of sense. Ego,
memory, other faces moving in and out of range,
a little knowledge, pain, a little wisdom, sympathy.
I receive, deceived or true: reflexive am I.

I hear and obey, attack or defend to save, this.
Have I harmed, helped, fought where words can go?
How do I know? —other voices, angels, gargoyles.
I am god, I am demon, can love, be loved; it is good
when I feel shame, it is good when I feel love (such

great fortune, that one thing you did not win but
took it when it came). But I am secretly in love with
war, Adam at play outside the gates, having made
his choice, scorning Eve's knowledge of loss. Then, a
momentary insight: almost aware that blood and mind
are much too flushed with clash of fear and pride for understanding,
I see it is time to share the gift of fear.
But then, in place of charity, it enters by some other door
to which I quickly move the elusive knight! Someone
in me says, do not remove your hand and the knight can

be withdrawn. Volition needs spaces where silences are
flexed and filtered, spaces I know I do not know exist.
I sit at the loom and weave between tension and give;
and even so, I do not know how to read so many colors.

And here I dare dominion, fearing trust and love.

December, 2012

On a soft ledge by spumy tides
a man stands entranced. Waves'
eternally dying aims, world's birth
and death song played in steady
measure, cradle of endless dying.

He is drawn to its design, place of
reckoning. Know you, that was the
term that sailors used when wild
Atlantic's keen drew to dark graves.

A simple means of measurement,
dead reckoning, the way of men
whose lives are often touched by
clouds that blur their boundaries;
unruly ocean covers and contains.

How can one go thoughtless up the shore
where such soundings rise?

WHEN THREATENED BY A CAREER IN POLITICS

Why is it only sins accompany me?
Why not my supple victories, moments
on a stage where I played lead roles
or made an act of grace out of honesty's
subtle secretary at the inner office door.

Every man remembers public deeds,
though they fail to come as advocates
before the bar of night when dark reclaims:
remembrance and some synonym of pride
that still will not admit self-deceit. In time
none can be more alone than in the mesh
of his own mind, with honesty like acid-eating
peace, virtue turned inquisitor oblique.

Where are those who loved me then? Gone,
their forgotten taste of grape.

After Auden's "Musée des Beaux Arts"

The masters, passionate for war, were sure.
The many cheered them on, though mothers wept
             to see the young ones go.
One sunny day by consequence of Sunni fury
Private Icarus is blown skyward by a bomb,
his daring known, his death a failed adventure.
Inarticulate, amazed and gaping faces see
those shreds of color arc in a searing sky,
while over the span of sand and sea, gannets
             called more plaintively.
In Maine his father plowed a heavy snow,
senses bedded in dense white pain;
neighbors in their pickups passed him by
and each one lightly touched the horn.
About suffering, they were never wrong…

Other Poetry Collections
by Curt Curtin

<u>For Adults</u>

For Art's Sake

Kerry Dancers

Nature's Eclectic Designs

<u>For Children & Young Adults</u>

Why Trees Sneeze and Other Mysteries

So Much Depends on Where You Live

For more on Curt's work, please visit <u>www.curtcurtinpoet.com</u>